HUCKLEBERRY FINN

"I never had a home," writes Huck, "or went to school like all the other boys. I slept in the streets or in the woods, and I could do what I wanted, when I wanted. It was a fine life."

So when Huck goes to live with the Widow Douglas, he doesn't like it at all. He has to be clean and tidy, be good all the time, and go to school. Then his father comes and takes him away to live in the woods. At first Huck is pleased, but his father is always hitting him so Huck decides to run away.

When he meets Jim, a runaway slave, they decide to travel together down the great Mississippi River on a raft. They run into all kinds of trouble and danger, of course, but Huck is happy. Life on the river is free, easy, and comfortable …

OXFORD BOOKWORMS LIBRARY
Classics

Huckleberry Finn

Stage 2 (700 headwords)

Series Editor: Jennifer Bassett
Founder Editor: Tricia Hedge
Activities Editors: Jennifer Bassett and Alison Baxter

American Edition: Daphne Mackey, University of Washington

MARK TWAIN

The Adventures of
Huckleberry Finn

Retold by
Diane Mowat

Illustrated by
Paul Fisher Johnson

OXFORD UNIVERSITY PRESS

OXFORD
UNIVERSITY PRESS

Great Clarendon Street, Oxford OX2 6DP

Oxford University Press is a department of the University of Oxford.
It furthers the University's objective of excellence in research, scholarship,
and education by publishing worldwide in

Oxford New York

Auckland Cape Town Dar es Salaam Hong Kong Karachi
Kuala Lumpur Madrid Melbourne Mexico City Nairobi
New Delhi Shanghai Taipei Toronto

With offices in

Argentina Austria Brazil Chile Czech Republic France Greece
Guatemala Hungary Italy Japan Poland Portugal Singapore
South Korea Switzerland Thailand Turkey Ukraine Vietnam

OXFORD and OXFORD ENGLISH are registered trade marks of
Oxford University Press in the UK and in certain other countries

This edition © Oxford University Press 2007

Database right Oxford University Press (maker)

First published in Oxford Bookworms 1994

6 8 10 9 7 5

ISBN 978 0 19 423747 5

Printed in China

ACKNOWLEDGEMENTS
Map by: Judy Stevens

CONTENTS

1
Huck in Trouble

You don't know about me if you haven't read a book called *The Adventures of Tom Sawyer*. Mr. Mark Twain wrote the book, and most of it is true. In that book robbers stole some money and hid it in a very secret place in the woods. But Tom Sawyer and I found it, and after that we were rich. We got six thousand dollars each—all gold.

In those days I never had a home or went to school like Tom and all the other boys in St. Petersburg. Pop was always drunk, and he moved around a lot, so he wasn't a very good father. But it didn't matter to me. I slept in the streets or in the woods, and I could do what I wanted, when I wanted. It was a fine life.

I could do what I wanted, when I wanted. It was a fine life.

1

When we got all that money, Tom and I were famous for a while. Judge Thatcher, who was an important man in our town, kept my money in the bank for me. And the Widow Douglas took me to live in her house and said I could be her son. She was very nice and kind, but it was a hard life because I had to wear new clothes and be good all the time.

In the end, I put on my old clothes and ran away. But Tom came after me and said that I had to go back, but that I could be in his gang of robbers. So I went back, and the widow cried, and I had to put on those new clothes again. I didn't like it at all. Her sister, Miss Watson, lived there too. She was always saying, "Don't put your feet there, Huckleberry," and "Don't do that, Huckleberry." It was terrible.

When I went up to bed that night, I sat down in a chair by the window. I sat there a good long time, and I was really unhappy. But just after midnight I heard "mee-yow! mee-yow!" outside. Very softly, I answered, "mee-yow! mee-yow!" Quietly, I put out the light and got out through the window. In the trees, Tom Sawyer was waiting for me.

We went through the trees to the end of the widow's garden. Soon we were on top of a hill on the other side of the house. Below us we could see the river and the town. One or two lights were still on, but everything was quiet. We went down the hill and found Joe Harper, Ben Rogers, and two or three more of the boys. Then Tom took us down the river by boat to his secret place, which was a cave deep in the side of a hill. When we got there, Tom told us all his plan.

"Now, we'll have this gang of robbers," he said, "and we'll call it Tom Sawyer's Gang. If somebody hurts one of us, the others will kill him and his family. And if a boy from

Tom's secret place was a cave, deep in the side of a hill.

the gang tells other people our secrets, we'll kill him and his family, too."

We all thought this was wonderful, and we wrote our names in blood from our fingers. Then Ben Rogers said, "Now, what's the gang going to do?"

"Nothing," replied Tom. "Just rob and kill. We stop people on the road, and we kill them and take their money and things. But we can keep a few of the people, and then their friends can pay money to get them back. That's what they do in the stories in books."

But Ben wasn't happy. "What about women?" he asked. "Do we kill them, too?"

"Oh, no," Tom answered. "We're very nice to them, and they all love us. They don't want to go home."

"Then the cave will be full of women and people waiting, and we'll have to watch them all night..."

"We'll all go home now," Tom said, "and we'll meet next week. Then we'll kill and rob somebody."

Ben wanted to begin on Sunday, but the others said no. It was bad to kill and rob on a Sunday.

My clothes were very dirty, and I was very tired when I got back. Of course, the next morning Miss Watson was angry with me because of my dirty clothes, but the widow just looked unhappy. Soon after that we stopped playing robbers because we never robbed people and we never killed them.

* * *

Miss Watson was angry, but the widow just looked unhappy.

Time went on, and winter came. I went to school most of
the time, and I was learning to read and write a little. It
wasn't too bad, and the widow was pleased with me. Miss
Watson had a slave, an old man called Jim, and he and I
were good friends. I often sat talking to Jim, but I still didn't
like living in a house and sleeping in a bed.

Then, one morning, there was some new snow on the ground and outside the back garden I could see footprints in the snow. I went out to look at them more carefully. They were Pop's footprints!

They were Pop's footprints!

A minute later, I was running down the hill to Judge Thatcher's house. When he opened the door, I cried, "Sir, I want you to take all my money. I want to give it to you."

He looked surprised. "Why, what's the matter?"

"Please, sir, take it! Don't ask me why!"

In the end he said, "Well, you can sell it to me, then." And he gave me a dollar, and I wrote my name on a piece of paper for him.

That night when I went up to my room, Pop was sitting there, waiting for me! I saw that the window was open, so that was how he got in.

He was almost fifty, and he looked old. His hair was long and dirty, and his face was a terrible white color. His clothes were old and dirty, too, and two of his toes were coming through his shoe. He looked at me all over for a long time, and then he said, "Well, just look at those clean, tidy clothes! And they say you can read and write now. Who said you could go to school?"

"The widow…" I began.

"Oh, she did, did she? Well, you can forget about school. I can't read, and your mother couldn't read; no one in our family could read before they died, so who do you think you are? Go on, take that book and read to me!"

I began to read, but he hit the book, and it flew out of my hand, across the room. Then he shouted, "They say you're rich—how's that?"

"It isn't true!"

"You give me that money! I want it. Get it for me tomorrow!"

"I haven't got any money. Ask Judge Thatcher. He'll tell you. I haven't got any money."

"Well, give me what you've got in your pocket now. Come on, give it to me!"

"I've only got a dollar, and I want that to..."

"Give it to me, do you hear?"

He took it, and then he said he was going out to get a drink. When he was outside the window, he put his head back in and shouted, "And stop going to that school, or you know what you'll get!"

The next day he was drunk, and he went to Judge Thatcher to get my money. The judge wouldn't give it to him. But Pop didn't stop trying, and every few days I got two or three dollars from the judge to stop Pop from hitting me. But when Pop had money, he got drunk again and made trouble in town. He was always coming to the widow's house, and she got angry and told him to stay away. Then Pop got really angry, and one day he caught me and took me a long way up the river in a boat. I had to stay with him in a hut in the woods, and I couldn't go out by myself. He watched me all the time. The widow sent a man to find me and bring me home, but Pop went after him with a gun, and the man ran away.

I had to stay with him in a hut in the woods.

2
Huck Escapes and Finds a Friend

Mostly it was a lazy, comfortable kind of life, but after about two months Pop began to hit me too much with his stick. He often went away into town too, and then he always locked me in the hut. Once he was away for three days, and I thought I was never going to get out again.

When he came back that time, he was drunk and angry. He wanted my money, but Judge Thatcher wouldn't give it to him. The judge wanted to send me to live with the widow again, Pop told me. I wasn't very pleased about that. I didn't want to go back there.

So I decided to escape and go down the river and live in the woods somewhere. When Pop was out, I began to cut a hole in the wooden wall of the hut. In a few days, when the hole was bigger, I could take the wood out, escape through the hole, and put the wood back.

One morning Pop sent me down to the river to catch some fish for breakfast. To my surprise, there was a canoe in the water, and there was no one in it. Immediately, I jumped into the river and brought the canoe to the side. It was lucky that Pop didn't see me, and I decided to hide the canoe under some trees and use it when I escaped.

That afternoon, Pop locked me in and went off to town.

I jumped into the river and brought the canoe to the side.

"He won't be back tonight," I thought, so I began to work hard at my hole, and soon I was outside. I ran down to the canoe with some food, drink, and Papa's gun. Then I ran back to the hut and put back the wood to hide the hole. I took the gun and went into the woods. There I shot a wild pig and took it back to the hut. Then I broke down the door with an ax and carried the pig in. I put some of its blood on the ground, and then I put some big stones in a sack and pulled it along behind me to the river. Last of all, I put some

I broke down the door with an ax.

blood and some of my hair on the ax. I left the ax in a corner of the hut and took the pig down to the river.

"They won't know it's only a pig in the river," I said to myself. "They'll think it's me."

Then I took the canoe and went down the river to Jackson's Island. By then it was nearly dark, so I hid the canoe under some trees and went to sleep.

It was after eight o'clock when I woke up the next day, and the sun was high in the sky. I was warm and comfortable, and I didn't want to get up. Suddenly, I heard a noise up the river. Carefully, I looked through the trees, and I saw a boat full of people. There was Pop, Judge Thatcher, Tom Sawyer, his Aunt Polly, his brother Sid, and lots of others. They were looking for my body in the river. I watched them, but they didn't see me, and in the end they went away. I knew that nobody was going to come and look for me again. I found a good place under the trees to sleep and to put my things. Then I caught a fish and cooked it over a fire.

I lived like that for three days, and then I decided to have a look around the island. So I went into the woods. "This is my island," I thought. "I'm the only person on it."

Suddenly, just in front of me, I saw a fire, and it was still smoking. There was somebody on my island! I didn't wait. I turned and went straight back. But I couldn't sleep. After a time, I said to myself, "I can't live like this. I must find out who it is."

Silently, I moved along the river in my canoe, under the darkness of the trees. And then I stopped. Through the trees I could see the light of a fire. Afraid, I left my canoe and went nearer. There was a man lying by the fire. Suddenly, he sat up and I saw that it was Jim, Miss Watson's slave! I was really happy to see him! "Hello, Jim," I cried, and I jumped out from behind the tree.

Jim fell to his knees. "Please don't hurt me!" he cried. "I've always been good to dead people!"

Jim fell to his knees. "Please don't hurt me!" he cried.

"It's all right, Jim. I'm not dead," I said. "But why are you here on the island?" I asked.

"Well, Huck," he began. "Old Miss Watson wanted to sell me. A man came into town and told Miss Watson that he'd buy me for eight hundred dollars. She couldn't say no, so I ran away. I ran down to the river to hide, but everybody in the town was there. They said you were dead, Huck. I had to wait all day to get away. When it was dark, I got on to a big boat and hid. When we came near this island, I jumped into the water and swam here."

Jim finished his story, and then we both carried all our things into a cave and hid the canoe under some trees. We were just in time because then the rains came. It rained for days, and the river got higher and higher. All kinds of things came down the river and one night there was a little wooden house, lying half on its side. We got the canoe out and went to take a look. Through the window we could see a bed, two old chairs, and some old clothes. There was something lying in the corner, and we thought it looked like a man. Jim went in to see, but he said, "He's dead. Someone shot him in the back. Don't look at his face, Huck. It's terrible!"

I didn't want to see the dead man's face, so I didn't look. We just took the old clothes and a few other things and went back to our cave on the island.

Another night, when we were out looking for things on the river, we found a raft. It was made of good, strong wood, and was about twelve feet by sixteen feet. "This could be useful," I said to Jim, so we pulled it back to the island behind the canoe and tied it up under the trees.

We tied the raft up under the trees.

3
Huck and Jim Travel South

For some days everything went along quietly, but we were getting bored. We wanted to know what was happening in town, and so I decided to go and find out. Jim said, "Why don't you wear the old dress and the hat that we found in the house? People won't know you, then. They'll think you're a girl." And so I did.

Just after it was dark, I got into the canoe and went up the river to the bottom of the town. There, I left the canoe and went on foot. Before long, I came to a little house which was always empty. Now there was a light on, and when I looked through the window, I saw a woman of about forty. She was a stranger, and that was good because she didn't know me. So I knocked on the door. "I have to remember that I'm a girl," I said to myself.

The woman opened the door. "Come in," she said. She looked at me with her little bright eyes. "What's your name?" she asked.

"Sarah Williams," I replied. "I'm going to see my uncle, on the other side of town. My mother's ill, you see, and she needs help."

"Well, you can't go there by yourself now. It's too dark. My husband will be home in about an hour. Wait for him, and he'll walk with you."

And then she began to tell me about all her troubles. I was getting bored with all this until she said something about Pop and my murder.

"Who did it?" I asked.

"Well," she replied, "some people say old Finn did it himself; other people think it was a slave who ran away that night. His name was Jim. They'll give three hundred dollars to anybody who finds him—and they'll give two hundred dollars for old Finn. He got drunk and left town with two strangers. A lot of people think he killed his boy and he's going to come back one day and get all Huck Finn's money."

"And what about the slave?" I asked.

"Oh, they'll soon catch him. People want the three hundred dollars. I think he's on Jackson's Island, you know. I've seen smoke there. My husband's gone to get two of his friends, and they're going over there with a gun later tonight."

When I heard this, my hands began to shake. The woman looked at me strangely, but then she smiled and said kindly, "What did you say your name was?"

"M—Mary Williams."

"Oh," she said, "I thought it was Sarah."

"Er... well, yes, it is. Sarah Mary Williams. Some people call me Sarah, and some people call me Mary, you see."

"Oh, do they?" She smiled again. "Come on, now—what's your real name? Bill? Bob? I know you're not really a girl."

So then I had to tell her another story, with a different name, and I said I was running away. She said she wouldn't tell anybody, and gave me some food before I left. I hurried back to the island and Jim.

"Quick, Jim!" I cried, waking him up. "They're coming to get us!"

We got out the raft as fast as we could, put all our things on it, tied the canoe on behind, and moved off down the

river. When it began to get light, we hid. When it was dark again, we traveled on. On the fifth night we passed St. Louis, and we decided to go on down to Cairo in Illinois, sell the raft there, and get a boat to Ohio. There are no slaves in Ohio.

We slept for most of that day, and we began our journey again when it was dark. After some time, we saw lights on the Illinois side of the river, and Jim got very excited. He thought it was Cairo. Jim got the canoe ready, and I went off in it to take a look at those lights. But it wasn't Cairo.

After that, we went on down the river. It was very dark that night, and it wasn't easy to see where we were going. Suddenly, a big steamboat came at us very fast, and the next minute it was right over us. Jim and I jumped off the raft into the water. The boat hit the raft and went on up the river.

When I came up out of the water, I couldn't see Jim anywhere. I called out his name again and again, but there was no answer. "He's dead!" I thought. Slowly, I swam to the side of the river and got out. I saw that I was near a big old wooden house. Suddenly a lot of very angry dogs jumped out at me. They made a terrible noise, and someone called from the house, "Who's there?"

"George Jackson," I answered quickly. "I've fallen off a river boat."

Well, the people who lived in that house were very kind, and they took me in and gave me some new clothes and a

The next minute the steamboat was right over us.

good meal. I told them that my family were all dead, so they said I could stay with them as long as I wanted. It was a beautiful house, and the food was good there, so I stayed.

A few days later one of the slaves in the house came to me and said, "Come with me!" Together, we went down to some trees by the river. "In there!" he said, and went away.

21

On the ground, I found a man, asleep. It was Jim! I was really pleased to see him. When the steamboat hit the raft, Jim told me, the raft didn't break up. Jim swam after it and caught it. Then he began to look for me.

We decided to leave at once. It's all right living in a house for a little while, but you feel more free and easy and comfortable on a raft.

4

The Duke and the King

Two or three days and nights went by, and nothing much happened. We traveled at night when it was dark and everybody was asleep. We didn't want anyone to see Jim and ask questions about him.

Then, one morning, just after it was light, I found a little canoe, so I got into it and went over to the side of the river. I was looking around when, suddenly, two men ran through the trees.

"Help!" they cried. "There are men and dogs trying to catch us. But we've done nothing wrong!"

One of the men was about seventy years old; the other was about thirty, and they both had very old, dirty clothes.

I said they could come with me, and we ran quickly back to the canoe.

Back on the raft we talked for a time, and then the young man said, "My friends, I think I can tell you my secret now. I'm really a duke. My grandfather was the son of the Duke of Bridgewater, but he left England and came to America. When the old Duke died, my grandfather's younger brother stole everything and made himself the Duke of Bridgewater."

Well, of course, we were all very unhappy for our friend the Duke, but he said, "I'll be happier if you do things for me. Bring me my dinner!"

So we did things for him, and he liked it. But the old man

"Bring me my dinner!" said the Duke.

23

spoke very little, and he looked unhappy, too. After a time he said, "You know, Bridgewater, I, too, have a secret." And he began to cry.

"What do you mean?" the Duke asked. "What's your secret?"

And then the old man told us that he was really the first son of the King of France. He asked us all to go down on one knee when we spoke to him. We could call him "Your Majesty," too. So that was what we did, and they were both happy. Of course, I knew that they weren't really a duke and a king, but I didn't tell Jim. It's best if everybody is happy when you're living together on a raft.

The King and the Duke were very interested in Jim. "Is he a slave?" they wanted to know. "Is he running away?"

I had to tell them something, so I said that Jim belonged to my uncle and was taking me to my family in New Orleans.

"Well, we'll travel down river with you, then," said the King. "We'll have a fine time together."

So the four of us went on down the river, but Jim and I didn't like those two men. They were always getting drunk and making plans to get money out of people in every town. It's all right to take a chicken or something if you're hungry, but these men were really bad! Jim and I decided to get away from them as soon as we could. It wasn't easy because they wanted to be with us all the time.

Then one morning the King went off into a town and told

us to wait for him. We waited all morning, and he didn't come back, so the Duke and I went into town to look for him. We looked all afternoon, and in the end we found him in a bar, drunk, and then he and the Duke began to fight about some money.

"Now we can get away from them," I thought. I turned

We found the King in a bar, drunk.

25

and ran back to the river. "Quick, Jim!" I shouted. "It's time to go!" But there was no answer. Jim wasn't there!

I ran into the woods, crying and shouting Jim's name. But there was still no answer.

Just then a boy came along. "Have you seen a slave?" I asked him, and I described Jim.

"Why, yes," the boy replied. "He's a runaway slave. I heard all about it in town. A family called the Phelpses have got him now. An old man in a bar told Mr. Phelps that there was a runaway slave on a raft down by the river. He said he didn't have time to take the slave back himself. So Mr. Phelps gave him forty dollars, and they went down and caught the slave this afternoon. The Phelpses are going to take him back to his owner, and they'll get three hundred dollars for him!"

I knew those two men were bad! I asked the boy where the Phelpses lived, and he said it was a big white house a little way down the river.

I began to make plans to get Jim back. First, I took the raft and went down to a little island. I hid the raft under the trees and lay down to sleep. Before it was light, I went off down the river in the canoe. When I thought I was near the Phelpses' place, I stopped, got out of the canoe and went up to the house. Suddenly, a lot of dogs ran out. They came from everywhere, and they made a terrible noise.

A woman about fifty years old ran out of the house, with

some little children behind her. She was smiling all over her face, and she took me by the hands and cried, "It's you, at last, isn't it?"

I didn't stop to think. "Yes, ma'am," I said.

She was smiling all over her face.

"Well, what took you so long? We thought you were coming two days ago. Your Uncle Silas goes to town every day to meet you. He's there now, but he'll be back soon." She didn't stop talking, and I couldn't tell her that she was making a mistake. "Tell us all about them," she cried. "Tell me everything."

I knew then that I had to tell her... but just then she cried, "Here he is! Quick, hide!" and she pushed me inside the house and behind the front door. Then her husband came in, and she asked him, "Has he come?"

"No," her husband replied.

"Look!" she shouted, and then she pulled me out from behind the door.

"Why, who's that?" Mr. Phelps cried, surprised.

"It's Tom Sawyer!" she laughed.

5

The Plan to Free Jim

When I heard that, I nearly fell through the floor, but it was a big piece of luck. It was easy for me to be Tom Sawyer because Tom was my best friend. He and his brother Sid lived with their Aunt Polly up in St. Petersburg, and I knew all about them. Now I learned that Aunt Polly had a sister, who was Mrs. Phelps. She and her husband were Tom's Aunt Sally and Uncle Silas. And Tom was coming down south by boat to stay with them for a bit.

We all sat there talking, and I could answer all their questions about the Sawyer family. I was feeling really

We all sat there talking, and I could answer all their questions.

happy about this when suddenly I heard a boat on the river. "Tom could be on that boat," I thought, "and he's going to walk in here and call out my name before I can stop him. I've got to go and meet him."

So I told the Phelpses that I would go into town to get my bags, which were at the boat station. I hurried up the road, and before I was halfway to town, there was Tom Sawyer coming along.

When he saw me, his mouth fell open, and he looked a bit white in the face. "Aren't you dead?" he said. "Everybody said that you were murdered!"

"I'm not dead yet," I said, "but listen..." I told him about my adventures, and Tom loved all that. Then I told him about the Phelpses and that they thought I was Tom Sawyer. "What shall we do?" I asked him.

Tom thought for a bit, and then he said, "I know. You take my bags and say they're yours. I'll come to the house in about half an hour."

"All right," I said, "but there's another thing. You know old Miss Watson's slave Jim, who ran away? Well, he's a prisoner here, and I'm going to help him escape."

Before I was halfway to town, there was
Tom Sawyer coming along.

31

"Jim?" Tom said. "But he's—" Then he stopped and thought. "Right. I'll help, too. I'll make a really good plan." He looked very excited.

So I went back to the house with the bags, and Tom came along half an hour later. He knocked on the door, and when his Aunt Sally opened it, he said he was Sid, Tom's brother. He wanted his visit to be a surprise for his dear old Aunt Sally, he said.

Well, Aunt Sally was very pleased to see Tom *and* Sid. She thought it was wonderful. She and Uncle Silas were really nice people.

When we were alone later, Tom and I talked about Jim's escape. I said I had a plan, and Tom listened to it.

"It's a good plan," he said when I finished. "But it's too easy! It's got to be a real escape, like a real adventure in a story-book. So we want something difficult and dangerous. Now, listen to this..."

So he told me his plan. I knew it would be a good one because Tom's plans are always crazy and exciting.

And we sure had a lot of fun with that plan! We knew that Jim was locked up in a hut outside the house. Every night we got out through our bedroom window and dug a hole right under the wall of the hut. It took us a week, and it was hard work. We talked to Jim secretly and told him about the plan, and he was really pleased.

We also wrote secret letters to everybody. Tom said that

We dug a hole right under the wall of the hut.

people always do this in books. We wrote that there was a gang of slave-thieves coming up from the south. They wanted to steal Jim and get the three hundred dollars from his owner. Well, the Phelpses and their friends got very excited, and on the night of the escape I went into the sitting-room, and there was a crowd of men in there—all with guns!

I ran and told Tom, and he said that this was really good. "It's a real adventure now, all right," he said, very excited. "Perhaps they'll come after us, and shoot, and we'll all get killed!"

Well, there wasn't time to think about it because it all happened so quickly. We got Jim out through the hole under the wall and began to run down to the river. But the men heard us and came after us. They began to shoot, and so we ran as fast as we could to the canoe. We got in it and went over to Spanish Island. My raft was there, and our plan was to escape on that and go on down river.

We ran as fast as we could to the canoe.

"Now, Jim," I cried, "you're a free man!" We were all very happy, but Tom was the happiest of all because he had a bullet in his leg.

When Jim and I heard that, we weren't so happy. Tom wanted the adventure to go on, but Jim and I said that a doctor must look at Tom's leg. Tom was getting angry about this, but Jim said:

"You listen to me, Tom Sawyer. You say I'm a free man now, and perhaps I am. But old Jim is not going to run away and leave one of his friends with a bullet in his leg! So I'm staying right here until a doctor comes."

I knew Jim would say that. He was a good, true friend, and you can't say that about many people.

Well, that was the end of the adventure, really. I went and found a doctor in the town. He was a kind old man, and he said he would go over to the island. But Tom's leg got very bad, and the next day the doctor and some other men carried Tom home to the Phelpses' house. They brought Jim too, and they locked him up in the hut again. But the doctor said, "Be kind to him, because he didn't run away, and he stayed to help me with the boy."

They took Tom up to bed because his leg was really bad, and Aunt Sally sat with him while he slept. I didn't want to answer any questions, so I kept out of everybody's way.

When Tom woke up the next day, he felt better. I was in the room and he said to me, "Jim's all right, isn't he?"

They carried Tom home to the Phelpses' house—and they brought Jim too.

I didn't know what to say because Aunt Sally was listening, and before I could stop him, Tom went on:

"We did it, Aunt Sally. Me and Tom here. We helped Jim escape." He told her all about the digging and everything, and Aunt Sally's mouth was opening and closing like a fish. Then she got really angry with Tom.

"That slave is locked up again, and he's going to stay there. And if I catch you again—"

Tom suddenly sat up in bed. "You can't do that!" he cried. "Jim was old Miss Watson's slave, but she died two months ago. Before she died, she wrote that she wanted Jim to be free, and not a slave anymore. Jim's a free man, not a slave!"

Well, that was a surprise to me and Aunt Sally! She thought Tom was crazy. "But Sid, why did you help him to escape, if he was free already?" she said.

"I wanted the *adventure*, of course!" said Tom. "We made a really exciting plan and ... Oh my! ... AUNT POLLY!"

We turned around, and there was Tom's Aunt Polly in the doorway! That was the second big surprise. Aunt Sally was really pleased to see her sister and jumped up to put her arms around her. I got under the bed as fast as I could. There was trouble coming for me and Tom, that was for sure.

Then Aunt Polly said to Tom, "You always were a terrible boy, Tom Sawyer, and I want to know—"

"But Polly dear," said Aunt Sally, "this isn't Tom. It's Sid. Tom was here a minute ago. Where is he?"

"Where's Huck Finn, you mean," replied Aunt Polly. "Come out from under that bed, Huck Finn."

"Come out from under that bed, Huck Finn."

So Tom and I had to explain everything. Aunt Polly said that Aunt Sally wrote and told her that Tom and Sid were there. She knew that it wasn't true, so she decided to come and find out what was happening. But she said that it was true about Miss Watson and that Jim was a free man now.

We got Jim out of the hut, and Aunt Sally and Uncle Silas were really nice to him. Later, Tom, Jim, and I had a long talk

"Let's go and have adventures in the
wild country down south."

40

by ourselves. Tom talked and talked, and then he said, "Let's all three of us run away one night, and go and have adventures in the wild country down south."

It sounded like a good plan to me. "The only thing is," I said, "I don't have any money to buy the right clothes and things. All my money back in St. Petersburg will be in Pop's pockets by now."

"No," said Tom. "Your money's all there. Your Pop never came back."

"No, and he won't come back, Huck," Jim said. "You remember that dead man on the river, when I said 'Don't look at his face'? Well, that was your Pop. You can get your money when you want."

Tom's leg is almost better now, and I haven't got any more to write about. I'm really pleased about that because it was very difficult to write a book, and I won't do it again. But I think I'm going to have to run away before the others, because Aunt Sally wants me to live with her. I'll have to sleep in a bed and wear clean clothes and learn to be good, and I can't do that again. I've done it once already.

The End

Yours truly,

Huck Finn

GLOSSARY

bullet   you fire this from a gun

clean   not dirty

crazy   not knowing what you are doing

drunk   with too much alcohol inside you

duke   a man who is the head of a very important family in
Britain

gang   a group of people who sometimes do bad things together

judge   someone who decides if a person is a criminal or not

lie *(n)*   something you say that is not true

Majesty   you call a king "Your Majesty" when you speak to him

owner   the person something or someone belongs to

Pop   a word for father

rob   to steal

robber   someone who steals

slave   a person who belongs to someone and has to work, but
gets no money

widow   a woman whose husband is dead

Huckleberry Finn

ACTIVITIES

Before Reading

1 Read the back cover and the story introduction on the first page of the book. What do you know now about *Huckleberry Finn*? Check one box each time.

	YES	NO
1 Huck liked school.	☐	☐
2 Huck went to live with a woman called Widow Douglas.	☐	☐
3 Huck's father was kind to him.	☐	☐
4 Huck ran away.	☐	☐
5 Huck's friend Jim was a slave.	☐	☐
6 Huck and Jim traveled down the Mississippi.	☐	☐
7 Jim had 300 dollars.	☐	☐

2 What is going to happen in the story? Can you guess? Check one box for each sentence.

	YES	NO
1 Huck goes back to live with the Widow Douglas.	☐	☐
2 Huck's father dies.	☐	☐
3 Huck and Jim find a lot of money.	☐	☐
4 Huck and Jim fall in the river.	☐	☐
5 Huck and Jim meet some bad men.	☐	☐
6 Jim goes back to his owner.	☐	☐

While Reading

Read Chapter 1. Answer these questions.

1 How much money did Huck and his friend Tom have?
2 Why wasn't Huck's father a good father?
3 Why didn't Huck like living with the Widow Douglas?
4 Who was Miss Watson?
5 What was Tom's gang going to do?
6 Why did the gang stop playing robbers?
7 Who did Jim belong to?
8 Why did Huck give his money to Judge Thatcher?
9 Why did Huck's father want money?
10 Where did Huck's father take him?

Read Chapter 2. Put these sentences in the correct order.

1 Then one night, Huck found Jim lying by a fire.
2 Huck's father locked him in the hut.
3 Huck lived alone on the island for three days.
4 But Huck got out through a hole in the wall of the hut.
5 Another night, Huck and Jim found a raft in the river.
6 After that, Huck went to Jackson's Island in a canoe.
7 After the rains, Huck and Jim saw a dead man in the river.
8 Then Huck shot a pig and put its blood in the hut.

Read Chapter 3. Are these sentences true (T) or false (F)? Rewrite the false ones with the correct information.

1 Huck put a girl's dress and hat on.
2 The woman in the little house knew Huck.
3 People in the town believed that Huck was dead.
4 If someone catches Jim, they will get five hundred dollars.
5 The woman knew that Huck wasn't really a girl.
6 Huck and Jim wanted to go to Ohio.
7 The steamboat hit Huck and Jim.
8 The people in the big, old house were kind to Huck.
9 The raft broke up when the steamboat hit it.
10 Jim and Huck decided to stay with the people in the big house.

Read Chapter 4. Who said this, and to whom?

1 "There are men and dogs trying to catch us."
2 "I'm really a duke."
3 "We'll have a fine time together."
4 "It's time to go!"
5 "He's a runaway slave!"
6 "It's you, at last, isn't it?"
7 "It's Tom Sawyer!"

Before you read Chapter 5 (*The Plan to Free Jim*), can you guess what happens? Write Y (yes) or N (no) by each sentence.

1 Huck does not tell Mr. and Mrs. Phelps his name, and they believe that he is Tom Sawyer.
2 Tom Sawyer arrives and says that he is Huck Finn.
3 Tom and Huck make a hole under the wall of the hut.
4 Jim runs away, and the boys never see him again.
5 Someone shoots Jim.
6 Jim is sent back to Miss Watson, and the Phelpses get three hundred dollars.
7 Jim becomes a free man.

Read Chapter 5. Choose the best question-word for these questions, and then answer them.

Who / Why / Where

1 . . . did Tom and his brother Sid live?
2 . . . was Mrs. Phelps's sister?
3 . . . was Tom surprised to see Huck?
4 . . . did Tom tell Mrs. Phelps that he was?
5 . . . didn't Tom like Huck's plan to help Jim?
6 . . . was Jim locked up?
7 . . . did Tom and Huck write secret letters to everybody?
8 . . . was Tom happy when they got in the canoe?
9 . . . was Jim a free man?
10 . . . was the dead man in the river?

After Reading

1 Huck made people think that he was dead. Imagine that Huck's father told Judge Thatcher what he found at his hut. Fill in the gaps using these words.

ax, blood, broken, door, floor, ground, hair, killed, pulled, river

When I came back from town, the _____ of the hut was _____. I went inside and saw _____ on the _____ , and there was an _____ in the corner. I think that someone came to the hut and _____ Huck with the ax, because there was blood and _____ on it. Then they _____ his body along the _____ to the _____.

2 Put these words into two groups: words about the river and words about adventure. Then choose two words from each list and use them in sentences of your own.

river	adventure

bullet, canoe, fish, gang, kill, raft, robbers, shoot, steal, steamboat, swim, water

3 Here is a new illustration for the story. Find the best place in the story to put the picture, and answer these questions.

The picture goes on page ____.
1 Who is looking through the window of the house?
2 Who is inside the house?
3 What is he looking at?

Now write a caption for the illustration.

Caption: _____

4 Tom told Huck his plan to free Jim. Here is their conversation, but it is in the wrong order. Write it out in the correct order and put in the speakers' names. Tom speaks first (number 3).

1 _____ "Letters? But what will we write in our letters?"

2 _____ "No, they won't. We'll do it at night."

3 _____ "Now, listen to this. Jim is locked up in a hut. We have to get him out."

4 _____ "Yes, but we'll tell him our plan. I know he'll be pleased. But we must make it really dangerous, like in a book."

5 _____ "They write secret letters."

6 _____ "We can run to the river, get into the canoe, and go to Spanish Island to get the raft."

7 _____ "But the Phelpses will see us."

8 _____ "Very exciting. But how will we escape if they're shooting at us?"

9 _____ "How are we going to do that?"

10 _____ "What do people do in books?"

11 _____ "We'll dig a hole under the wall of the hut."

12 _____ "Jim will hear us, won't he?"

13 _____ "We'll write that a gang of slave-thieves wants to steal Jim and get the money. Then they'll try to stop us. Perhaps they'll shoot us. Won't that be exciting?"

5 **People keep a lot of secrets and tell a lot of lies in this story. What things did people say or not say? Complete these sentences. Use as many words as you like.**

1 Jim didn't tell Huck that _____.
2 Huck told the woman in the little house that _____.
3 The Duke told Huck and Jim that _____.
4 The King told Huck and Jim that _____.
5 Huck didn't tell Jim that _____.
6 Huck told the Duke and the King that _____.
7 Huck told the people in the big old house that

_____.

8 Huck didn't tell Mrs. Phelps that _____.
9 Tom didn't tell Huck that _____.

6 **What do you think of the people in the story? Make sentences from the chart. Use as many words as you like to complete your sentences.**

Pop		bad	
Huck		brave	
Tom		clever	
Jim	was	crazy	because . . .
Miss Watson	were	dangerous	
Mr. and Mrs. Phelps		kind	
the Duke and the King		stupid	

Example: Pop was bad because he hit Huck.

51

ABOUT THE AUTHOR

Mark Twain's real name was Samuel Clemens. He was born in Florida, a town in Missouri, in 1835, and he then lived in Hannibal, Missouri. When he was twelve, his father died, and he went out to work. He began to write for his brother's newspaper, and later he wrote for newspapers in Nevada and California. From 1857 to 1861, he was a river-pilot, guiding river boats on the great Mississippi river. The name "Mark Twain" came from his life on the Mississippi. The river-pilots called out words like these to the captain of the boat, and "mark twain" meant that there were two fathoms of water (about twelve feet) under the boat.

He started to write books of stories in 1867 and became famous for making people laugh. *The Adventures of Tom Sawyer* (1876) and *Huckleberry Finn* (1884) are his two most famous books. Many of the people and places in these stories are from the years when Mark Twain was a boy in Hannibal (Hannibal is the town of St. Petersburg in this story).

Mark Twain wrote many books. Some of them were important, some not so important, and he traveled to many English-speaking countries, talking about his work. Sadly, he had money problems, and his wife and two of his three daughters died before him, so his life was difficult and unhappy when he was older. He died in 1910.

OXFORD BOOKWORMS LIBRARY

Classics • Crime & Mystery • Factfiles • Fantasy & Horror
Human Interest • Playscripts • Thriller & Adventure
True Stories • World Stories

The OXFORD BOOKWORMS LIBRARY provides enjoyable reading in English, with a wide range of classic and modern fiction, non-fiction, and plays. It includes original and adapted texts in seven carefully graded language stages which take learners from beginner to advanced level.

All Stage 1 titles, as well as over eighty other titles from Starter to Stage 6, are available as audio recordings. All Starters and many titles at Stages 1 to 4 are specially recommended for younger learners. Every Bookworm is illustrated, and Starters and Factfiles have full-color illustrations.

The OXFORD BOOKWORMS LIBRARY also offers extensive support. Each book contains an introduction to the story, notes about the author, a glossary, and activities. Additional resources include tests and worksheets, as well as answers for these and for the activities in the books. There is advice on running a class library, using audio recordings, and the many ways of using Oxford Bookworms in reading programs. Resource materials are available on the website <www.oup.com/bookworms>.

The *Oxford Bookworms Collection* is a series for advanced learners. It consists of volumes of short stories by well-known authors, both classic and modern. Texts are not abridged or adapted in any way, but carefully selected to be accessible to the advanced student.

You can find details and a full list of titles in the *Oxford Bookworms Library Catalog* and *Oxford English Language Teaching Catalogs*, and on the website <www.oup.com/bookworms>.

Robinson Crusoe

DANIEL DEFOE

Retold by Diane Mowat

"I often walked along the shore, and one day I saw something in the sand. I went over to look at it more carefully ... It was a footprint—the footprint of a man!"

In 1659 Robinson Crusoe was shipwrecked on a small island off the coast of South America. After fifteen years alone, he suddenly learns that there is another person on the island. But will this man be a friend—or an enemy?

New Yorkers

O. HENRY

Retold by Diane Mowat

A housewife, a tramp, a lawyer, a waitress, an actress—ordinary people living ordinary lives in New York at the beginning of this century. The city has changed greatly since that time, but its people are much the same. Some are rich, some are poor, some are happy, some are sad, some have found love, and some are looking for love.

O. Henry's famous short stories—sensitive, funny, sympathetic —give us vivid pictures of the everyday lives of these New Yorkers.

Dracula

BRAM STOKER

Retold by Diane Mowat

In the mountains of Transylvania there stands a castle. It is the home of Count Dracula—a dark, lonely place. At night the wolves howl around the walls...

In the year 1875 Jonathan Harker comes from England to do business with the Count. But Jonathan does not feel comfortable at Castle Dracula. Strange things happen at night, and very soon he begins to feel afraid. And he is right to be afraid because Count Dracula is one of the Un-Dead—a vampire that drinks the blood of living people...

Sherlock Holmes Short Stories

SIR ARTHUR CONAN DOYLE

Retold by Clare West

Sherlock Holmes is the greatest detective of them all. He sits in his room and smokes his pipe. He listens, watches, and thinks. He listens to the steps coming up the stairs; he watches the door opening—and he knows what question the stranger will ask.

In these three of his best stories, Holmes has three visitors to the famous apartment in Baker Street—visitors who bring their troubles to the only man in the world who can help them.

The Call of the Wild

JACK LONDON

Retold by Nick Bullard

When men find gold in the frozen north of Canada, they need dogs—big, strong dogs to pull the sleds on the long journeys to and from the gold mines.

Buck is stolen from his home in the south and sold as a sled-dog. He has to learn a new way of life—how to work in harness, how to stay alive in the ice and the snow ... and how to fight. Because when a dog falls down in a fight, he never gets up again.

A Christmas Carol

CHARLES DICKENS

Retold by Clare West

Christmas is humbug, Scrooge says just a time when you find yourself a year older and not a penny richer. The only thing that matters to Scrooge is business, and making money.

But on Christmas Eve three spirits come to visit him. They take him traveling on the wings of the night to see the shadows of Christmas past, present, and future—and Scrooge learns a lesson that he will never forget.